MW01101209

Variety of Life

Mammals

Please visit our web site at: www.garethstevens.com
For a free color catalog describing Gareth Stevens Publishing's
list of high-quality books and multimedia programs, call
1-800-542-2595 (USA) or 1-800-387-3178 (Canada).
Gareth Stevens Publishing's fax: (414) 332-3567.

Library of Congress Cataloging-in-Publication Data

Richardson, Joy.
    Mammals / Joy Richardson. — North American ed.
        p. cm. — (Variety of life)
    Includes bibliographical references and index.
    ISBN 0-8368-4506-4 (lib. bdg.)
    1. Mammals—Juvenile literature. I. Title.
  QL706.2.R534   2005
  599—dc22   2004058988

This North American edition first published in 2005 by
Gareth Stevens Publishing
A WRC Media Company
330 West Olive Street, Suite 100
Milwaukee, Wisconsin 53212 USA

This U.S. edition copyright © 2005 by Gareth Stevens, Inc.
Original editions copyright © 1993 and 2003 by Franklin Watts.
First published in 1993 by Franklin Watts, 96 Leonard Street,
London EC2A 4XD, England.

Franklin Watts Editors: Sarah Ridley and Sally Luck
Franklin Watts Designer: Janet Watson
Picture Research: Sarah Moule

Gareth Stevens Editor: Dorothy L. Gibbs
Gareth Stevens Designer: Kami Koenig

Picture credits: Bruce Coleman, Ltd. – 3, 7(top right, bottom right,
and bottom left), 11, 13, 15, 19, 23, 25; Frank Lane Picture Agency –
17, 21; Natural History Photographic Agency – cover, 7(top left), 9, 27.

All rights reserved. No part of this book may be reproduced, stored in
a retrieval system, or transmitted in any form or by any means, electronic,
mechanical, photocopying, recording, or otherwise, without the prior
written permission of the copyright holder.

Printed in the United States of America

1 2 3 4 5 6 7 8 9 09 08 07 06 05

Variety of LIFE

Joy Richardson

Mammals

GARETH STEVENS
GS
PUBLISHING
A WRC Media Company

Contents

Words that appear in the glossary are printed in **boldface** type the first time they occur in the text.

People Are Mammals

What do elephants, gorillas, whales, and bats have in common with people?

These animals do not look like people. They do not even look like each other, but their bodies all work in the same kinds of ways.

All of these animals, including people, belong to the group of animals called mammals.

Mammals are found on land, in the sea, and in the air.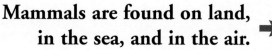

A Warm Place to Grow

Almost all baby mammals grow inside their mothers.

Unlike so many other kinds of animals, most mammals do not lay eggs to **reproduce**. Instead, mammals carry their growing babies inside their bodies. When the babies are ready to be born, they come out of their mother's bodies, fully **developed** and alive.

Baby elephants grow inside their mothers for almost two years. Baby hamsters grow inside their mothers for about two weeks.

Human mothers carry their babies inside them for nine months.

A calf grows inside its mother for nine months.

8

Growing Up

Some baby mammals grow up quickly. Others take a long time to grow.

A rabbit gives birth to lots of babies at the same time. The **newborn** rabbits are very small, and they cannot see or hear, but in only two or three months, they will be fully grown.

Human babies take much longer to grow up. They cannot even walk until they are about one year old.

Newborn rabbits have hardly any fur, and they cannot move around much, but they will grow very quickly.

An Unusual Start

Although most baby mammals grow inside their mothers until they are fully developed, a few start out in a more **unusual** way.

A kangaroo baby, which is called a joey, starts growing inside its mother. It is born when it is only about the size of a small caterpillar. Then it crawls around, through its mother's fur, into a **pouch** on the front of her body.

Inside its mother's pouch, the joey attaches itself to a **nipple** so it can drink its mother's milk. After about nine months of feeding and growing, it is ready to hop away on its own.

A joey first leaves its mother's pouch when it is six or seven months old, but it comes back to feed until it is nine or ten months old.

Milk to Drink

All baby mammals drink **milk** from their mothers. They need their mother's milk to grow and stay healthy.

The milk is made inside the mother's body. A baby drinks the milk by sucking on a nipple on the outside of the mother's body.

Some mammals give birth to many babies at one time. These mammals have lots of nipples so they can feed all of their babies at the same time.

A mother pig can have eight or more babies at one time, but she has many nipples on the underside of her body for feeding them.

New Foods

As young mammals grow, they stop drinking their mother's milk and start eating other kinds of foods.

Mammals such as cows and sheep are **herbivores**. They eat only plants.

Tigers and wolves and cats and dogs are **carnivores**. They eat mostly meat.

Humans are **omnivores**. They eat foods of all kinds.

Different mammals have different kinds of teeth for biting and chewing the foods they need.

A squirrel's sharp teeth can break open hard nutshells. ➡

Keeping Warm

All mammals are **warm-blooded** animals.

Because mammals have warm blood, the temperature of their bodies always stays the same, even when the temperature of their **surroundings** changes.

Sea mammals, such as seals, walrus, and polar bears, have a thick layer of **blubber** under their skin to help keep their bodies warm when they are swimming in icy water.

The layer of blubber under a seal's skin can be as much as 6 inches (15 centimeters) thick.

Hairy Bodies

All mammals have hair on their bodies, but some kinds of mammals have more hair than others.

Most dogs and cats are covered with thick hair or fur. Sheep also have thick hair, but sheep hair is called **wool** or **fleece**.

Humans are not very hairy, except on their heads. Humans are the only mammals who have to wear clothes to keep warm.

Its thick coat of wool keeps a lamb warm. People often wear wool sweaters to keep warm.

Legs, Arms, and Flippers

Most mammals have four legs. Mammals that have four legs can usually run very fast.

Cheetahs are the fastest runners in the world. A cheetah can run up to 70 miles (113 kilometers) per hour. A horse's top speed is less than 35 miles (56 km) per hour.

Mammals such as humans and gorillas have two legs and two arms. Two-legged mammals cannot run as fast as most four-legged animals, but they can do many other things with their arms and legs.

Sea mammals have **flippers** instead of legs, which makes them very good swimmers.

Orangutans use their arms and legs to swing from tree to tree.

Breathing

Like all animals, mammals need air to **breathe**. They breathe air into their **lungs**.

Most mammals live on land and breathe the same way humans do, but mammals that live underwater have to breathe a different way.

A whale is a sea mammal. When it wants to breathe, it swims to the **surface** of the water and breathes in air through a hole on the top of its head. Underwater, the whale holds its breath until it needs to come up for more air.

The hole on a whale's head is called a blowhole. When a whale breathes out, it blows a fountain of air and water into the sky. ➡

Flying Mammals

Bats are the only mammals with **wings**, and they are the only mammals that can fly.

Like other mammals, bats have furry bodies. Their heads look almost like little foxes. Even though they have wings, bats also have legs and arms. Their legs and arms are attached to their wings.

Bats have big ears and can hear very well. Their good hearing helps them when they are flying in the dark.

When bat babies are born, they **cling** to their mothers and drink their mothers' milk, just as other baby mammals do.

Most bats fly at night. ➡

Mammal Facts

There are all different kinds of mammals in the world, but they are the same in many ways.

- All mammals are warm-blooded animals.

- All mammals have hair or fur covering their bodies.

- All mammals drink milk from their mothers when they are babies.

- Most mammals have four legs.

For More Facts . . .

Books

Bats. Nature's Friends (series). Ann Heinrichs (Compass Point Books)

Explore and Discover Mammals. Question Time (series). Jim Bruce (Houghton Mifflin)

Mammals. Science Around Us (series). Peter Murray (Child's World)

What Is a Marine Mammal? The Science of Living Things (series). Bobbie D. Kalman (Crabtree)

Web Sites

All About Mammals
  www.kidzone.ws/animals/mammals.htm

bats4kids
  members.aol.com/bats4kids/

EEK! Critter Corner
  www.dnr.state.wi.us/org/caer/ce/eek/critter/mammal/

Glossary

blubber: a thick layer of fat under the skin of a sea mammal, such as a seal or a whale, which helps keep the animal's body warm when the temperature around the animal's body is cold

breathe: to inhale, or take in air, and exhale, or force out air, through lungs. All mammals breathe to get the oxygen their bodies need to stay alive.

carnivores: animals that feed mainly on the flesh, or meat, of other animals

cling: to hold onto tightly

developed: having grown to a natural shape and form with all necessary parts and pieces in place

fleece: the name used to describe the wool on the coats of animals such as sheep, goats, and llamas

flippers: the wide, flat, winglike parts near the front of a seal's body, which the animal uses as both arms and legs and which are especially good for swimming

herbivores: animals that feed only on plants

lungs: the spongy, baglike body parts in the chests of humans and most other mammals, which are used for breathing

milk: the nourishing liquid produced in the bodies of female mammals to feed their babies

newborn: newly or recently born; just brought to life through birth

nipple: the part of a female mammal's body through which the milk she produces is drawn, or brought out

omnivores: animals that eat both plant foods and meat

pouch: a kind of pocket on an animal's body, formed by loose or stretchy skin

reproduce: to have babies

surface: the top or outside layer of something

surroundings: all of the objects and conditions that are present in a particular place or area

unusual: uncommon; out of the ordinary

warm-blooded: having a body temperature that stays about the same no matter how warm or cold the air is around the body

wings: the armlike parts of a bird's or a bat's body that are used for flying

wool: the soft, thick, wavy or curly hair of animals such as sheep, goats, and llamas

Index